JUDAS
Hero Misunderstood

The Misunderstood Series

Jason E. Royle

Copyright © 2014 Jason E. Royle

All rights reserved worldwide

No part of this book/eBook may be made publicly available, reproduced, or copied/sold in any form whatsoever without the express written consent of the author.

Requests for permission should be addressed to:
J. E. Royle, Box 283, Schaefferstown, PA 17088
or emailed to roylejason@gmail.com.

Connect with Jason
www.twitter.com/JERoyle
www.amazon.com/author/jroyle

Contents

Opening Letter from the Author 1
Chapter 1 3
Chapter 2 9
Chapter 3 18
Chapter 4 28
Chapter 5 39
Closing Letter from the Author 43
It Is Written 44
The Devil Made Me Do It 47
The Betrayer(s) 49
The Way of Judas 51
Suicide in the Bible 53
The Last Supper Betrayal: What Really Happened? 58
Works Consulted 61

To those who are quick to judge

Judge not, lest ye be judged. For in the same way you judge others, you will be judged.

—Matthew 7:1-3

Opening Letter from the Author

Friend,

If you picked up this book hoping to find page after page of exhaustive critical analysis and scriptural interpretation on Judas Iscariot, I have a confession to make—that is not how this short story goes. For something like that I would recommend the Anchor or Word Biblical Commentary series.

What you have in your hands is historical fiction with a splash of possibility, a reframing, a different flavor, an imaginative retelling from the perspective of one of the most notorious characters in the Bible—Judas.

Moving forward, I am going to ask you to do something you may have never done before. I would like you to pull away from every judgment about Judas you might have and turn your attention instead to a different set of thoughts:

Have you said or ever heard someone say, "Everything has a purpose," or, "All of us have a purpose in life"? These statements inspired the questions being asked in this book about Judas: "Did Judas have a purpose? If so, what was it?" Have you ever stepped back far enough to consider the "big" picture beyond the evil legend? What he did, was it really a villainous act?

Now before you leap to your feet and scream "Heresy!" I ask you politely to refrain and carefully consider the dishonest things we all do: the thoughtless telling of a secret that betrays a friend, the slight twisting of the truth to keep your job, the tiny lies we tell our children to get them to do what we want. Take a second and think about a few dark secrets in your life that, were they to ever come out, would test the very fabric of the relationships you treasure most. We all fall short of perfection.

Against all adversity: reintroducing Judas.

With all due respect,
Jason E. Royle

Chapter 1

We judge ourselves by what we feel capable of doing, while others judge us by what we have already done.
–Henry Wadsworth Longfellow

You know my story. But here it is again.

I am the one who brought about the crucifixion. I am the one who handed over his friend. I am the one damned for all eternity. I am the most hated man in history. Vilified forever, I am the apostle who betrayed Jesus. And for centuries my name has stood for evil, treachery, and deceit—until now.

I've finally decided to speak out. "Why now, after all these years?" Because I've endured more bullying than any one person could handle. It's over. I'm at my wit's end. By my own hand, my time here on earth is about to end. I suspect a wretched destiny awaits me on the other side. But before I go, I want to be heard. Just once, I need someone to listen.

"Judge not lest ye be judged." I'm sure you've heard that warning before, and we both know who said it.

Here's another saying to ponder:

"Between the sands of time and tradition is a multitude of truths untold."

Well, I have such truths to share.

I know what you're thinking. You're doubtful. Scratch that. You don't believe me. Not one bit. And I get it. I understand why—my reputation—it precedes me. But bear with me. This won't take long because I don't have that long.

Hear me out. Walk with me.

***

I've been camped here for several days now, waiting, hoping to die. I'm too afraid to pray for death. I'm a little concerned, as anyone would be, over what awaits me in the afterlife. But I can't take being here anymore. This life is not for me.

I'm in the most fitting place, I think. The Valley of Hinnom, hell on earth they call it. Countless bodies are entombed in these stiff hills. Fire and death are everywhere, and yet I also see a great deal of life I never really noticed before. Wiry branches with dusty leaves pushing up from the dry, parched ground. I try not to take it as a sign. These bushes might have something to live for, but I don't seem to. The irony is I have come

CHAPTER 1

to see death as my great escape, a chance to start over.

The sun looks white at the warmest point of the day. It's unseasonably warm this spring. There is no breeze. No movement. Just an endless series of moments where the air is like warm breath upon my face, and the shift in temperature is camouflaged by the beats of anxiety across my chest.

I'm tired. No. I'm exhausted, in every sense of the word. I would give anything for relief, but death just won't come. My idea (and I believe it was a good one) was to try, by a process of confession and self-examination, to discover a reason, or at least an ounce of justification for my outrageous behavior. But the more I think about it, the more appalled and upset I become for what I've done.

I originally planned to leave a note behind to explain everything. But I found after several tries there wasn't enough room for me to say all I wanted to say, not on a yellow sticky note anyway. What I have to say can't be contained in a hand-scribbled note.

Right when it all went down, I wanted someone gentle and understanding who I could confide in, someone with whom I could share every detail of this abhorrent event. Someone who would not judge me or make me feel ashamed. But I have no one. Not anymore. The one man who would've understood… well…

I can only hope I'm not too flustered to piece this all together. I hope you're not too upset with me to listen. I must confess that what disturbs me most about the whole thing is not so much my shame or even the continued anger I evoke in the millions of people who hear my story. What upsets me the most is what a fool I've been for ever thinking of myself as a hero.

Heroes make the hard choices, right? They do whatever it takes to get the job done. Well, that's what I did. Heroes save lives…or at least have a hand in saving lives. From my perspective, that's what I thought I was doing. I may not be Superman, but I certainly don't think I'm the devil everyone makes me out to be either. But, without fail, every time someone talks about the greatest story ever told, every time someone takes pen in hand and puts it to paper, I am always, and I mean always portrayed as *the opposition*. But the way I see it, while I'm no hero, I am *the essential helper*.

Am I not?

Think about it. Take a step back for a moment. Don't dwell on my legacy. Or on how you feel about me or on what your parents and grandparents think about me. I'm not perfect, I know that. Hasn't anyone ever told you that a wise man looks at a situation and makes his own decisions? I simply have a different point of view.

CHAPTER 1

I'm not crazy, am I?
I'm not *pure* evil, am I?
No.
What I am is…misunderstood.

***

My friends, Peter, James, John, Matthew, and the others, were my whole life. They were everything to me. They were all I had. And Jesus, well, he was the one man in all Jerusalem who had the power to put an end to Roman rule. He was the one man who could lead us into a new era. Please try to understand: I didn't intend to betray him. I did not wish for any harm to come to him. Can you understand that? I doubt it.

I'm so heartbroken I can hardly bring myself to organize the series of events, but I can't seem to stop the mess of jumbled thoughts and images from entering my mind. My whole life I've been waiting, wondering whether my prayer to change the world would ever come true. I guess it didn't.

I've made my decision. I stand up and grab the rope, the one I've been working on for the past few days. It's noosed. It's heavy. It's perfect. I toss the heavy braid of itchy fibers over my shoulder and, leaving behind everything else at my makeshift camp site, start again up the hill. I've already pinpointed my destination—a large, old tree at the top of one of the cliffs. A scattering of small leaves and fruit are just starting to grow at the ends of its branches. The tree sits right at the edge of the hill, tipped a little toward the city below. It's one brave tree standing tall for the entire world to see, at least all of Jerusalem anyway. As long as my bruised and battered feet are able to maintain a reasonably swift pace up the hill, I will get to my destination before dark. By tomorrow morning there will be one more piece of fruit dangling from that tree.

Chapter 2

*When God ordains that you should die in the dark,
it means nothing that your father is a candle maker.*
—Spanish proverb

When I reach the tree, I bow my head to rest. I guess I should just suck it up and keep moving and get it over with. But my adrenaline still rushes. And my heart, anxiously pounding, is telling me to just pause for a moment, look around, and take one last deep breath. So I rest.

I made good time getting up the hill. As I sit in the grass beside the tree, I enjoy my very last sunset. I'm hungry, but it doesn't matter now. My feet are covered in dirt mixed with sweat. That doesn't matter much either. I look down the hill and out over the city and straight ahead to a horizon that looks like it begins just about where the city ends. To my right, in the subtle distance I see a child, a boy, zigzagging his way down the hill. A dog scampers behind him. I look to the left. No one else is around. And for a brief, mysterious moment, an ounce of confusion sets in. I have no idea from which direction the boy and dog came, nor do I know where they're going. I thought they were going down the hill. Now I'm not so sure. Isn't that something? Just as suddenly as they appeared, they disappeared.

I sit a little while longer. There's still no breeze, and if I'm not mistaken, still no change in the temperature. Without thinking, I tug at the knot on the rope to make sure it's secure then glance up at the tree to make a final decision on which branch to use. Finally, I'm on my feet and ready to get down to business—to do what I came to do. As I approach the tree, a gray rabbit hops across my line of site. Now why would a rabbit be in this Godforsaken place?

***

"Why would anyone hide out in this Godforsaken place?" one of the soldiers murmured on that fateful night when I led them to the place where Jesus was.

"Hide out?" another chimed in. "He's out in the open if he's at Gethsemane."

"That's because he's not hiding," I said, then considered my next words carefully. "He's…waiting."

In the clearing another few meters ahead I could see

CHAPTER 2

Peter sitting, reclined against the trunk of a tree. Beside him, John's head lay against his shoulder then popped up when the sound of our approach alerted the men to our presence. Peter was the first to his feet, and I turned my eyes from his glare as I made my way toward them so that I could do what needed to be done.

Jesus stood fearlessly in front of several of the disciples. I could hear them talking among themselves as I reached them and paused. My eyes scanned the faces of the three men with Jesus. I saw alarm, fear, and disappointment (if looks could kill…). Peter was the one I was worried about. He had the power to stop this whole thing from happening. Besides, he never did like me.

I looked at Jesus' face. I felt a little sad. But I also felt at peace. He tilted his head downward and then lifted his chin again ever so slightly, as if letting me know it was okay to come. So I did and gave him that now infamous kiss.

"Greetings, Rabbi." I had said those same two words hundreds of times before and it wasn't unusual for me to kiss him. But I had no idea that this kiss would be *the kiss*—the kiss that took me from being a regular guy to being the very personification of evil.

"Judas, are you betraying me with a kiss?" Jesus

asked and I pulled back from him slowly.

Betraying?

"Do what you came to do," he said.

His words threw me.

The chain of events that followed happened so fast the sequence gets cluttered in my mind. Peter moved toward us first and asked whether they should draw their swords. But before Jesus could answer, he'd already drawn his sword and sliced off the ear of one of the men who'd come to take Jesus. Quickly and forcefully, Jesus admonished Peter. "Peter!" he hollered in a way that temporarily silenced us all but stunned Peter. "You know better. Put your sword away. If you live by the sword, then you'll die by the sword."

Jesus stared at the ground for a moment, and for just a brief glimpse, the madness calmed as he picked the ear up off the ground and miraculously put it back on the head of the soldier who'd lost it.

Looking at us standing in awe Jesus said, "Don't you think that if I needed the help, I could call to my father and he would send thousands of angels to my rescue? But it's time. This is what the scriptures say must happen. Trust me. I know what I'm doing."

With that, Jesus looked at the temple guards. "You came for me with your weapons drawn. You've sat with

CHAPTER 2

me in the temple and learned at my feet and now you're coming for me like I'm a hardened criminal."

"Not coming for you," I heard one of the guards say.

"But placing you under arrest for your own protection," another added.

"That's right, Lord," I whispered.

"Nonsense," John cried out. "Nothing good can come of this arrest." Lunging forward, John was the first to make a move and stake his claim on Jesus. In the same instant, several of the soldiers took hold of Jesus and a fist fight broke out between the men who'd come for him and the disciples. I was stunned. So I stood there, watching the madness unfold.

Peter yelled out my name and hit me in the chest hard, ordering me to fight. "Fight for the Lord. Fight for freedom!" And I joined in the dangerous tussle for Jesus, except I was pulling him toward me, not toward either of the two groups fighting for him.

The soldiers quickly overpowered us. In the middle of the frightening, torch-lit scene, I could see they finally had Jesus in their custody. I watched as one of the guards brought Jesus' hands together and tied his wrists with rope. As they took him away Jesus looked back once, right at me. I'll take that look with me to the grave. He looked right through me, down to the darkest corridor of my heart, and left his mark. I knew in that moment, I would never see him again.

A remnant of men stayed behind to fight and fend off the small group of disciples. But we didn't stay. We ran to the place the other disciples were resting. When we got there, I was out of breath. I was trying to regain my composure when John came at me screaming and crying and hitting. "Judas! What did you do? With clinched fist he swung backward across my chest. "Tell me! What's going on?"

"You don't understand." I pushed him away and tugged hard on my clothes. "What I did—I did—I have my reasons. Besides, they only want to talk. The elders have a few questions they want to ask him. They want to know where he gets the authority to call himself a king. How he became popular so quickly. Who he has influenced. What his plans are. Jesus will be fine." I said those words in an attempt to convince myself. I needed someone to say he would be okay. "He's been up against the chief priests before. He handles himself well. You know that. Before daybreak he'll be…" I stammered on my words. I didn't believe them anymore. "Tomorrow…you'll see." I beat back a tear. "No harm will come to him. You'll see."

"What is this?" Thomas asked, taking long strides toward us. There was silence between us as the other

CHAPTER 2

disciples jumped to their feet.

"Where is Jesus?" I could hear everyone whisper in fear.

"They took him," Peter answered, pacing back and forth. Suddenly he ran toward me, knocked me over, and shoved my head against the ground.

"What? Who took him?" Thomas asked again but this time much more slowly. "*Judas…where…is…Jesus?*"

Still breathing hard from our skirmish with the guards, James motioned toward me and then spoke loud enough for all eleven men to hear: "Judas handed him over!"

***

I toss the rope over the top of the branch and catch it in my hand. "Where is Jesus?" I hear myself repeat out loud and my eyes well with tears. Why doesn't anyone get it? Even if his death didn't bring about the new kingdom he wanted or the revolution against Rome we needed, he still had to die. It was in the Bible. The Prophet Isaiah said it had to come to pass. The world would be reconciled to God through his death.

In the days before I went into hiding, I overheard people talking about what happened in the garden. The story was the same every time I heard it. It always ended with the stinging accusation that one of his followers handed him over to be scourged and crucified—but I didn't hand him over "to be scourged and crucified." I told the elders of his location because that's what I was supposed to do; I thought I was helping.

I tug on both ends of the rope, spooling the rope around each of my hands before lifting myself a few inches from the ground for a minute, with all my weight, to make sure the rope and the branch will hold. Behind me, the sound of creaking metal startles me and I twirl around to see what it could be. It's the first time I notice that I'm in an old, old cemetery with only a few dozen graves scattered here and there. My suicide tree is on the perimeter. I see now what was making the noise. On the far side of the cemetery is a narrow gate. It's metal.

There is no breeze but the gate keeps swinging, back and forth, as if beckoning me to come. Little by little I make my way to the gate and open it. Immediately the wind begins to howl, and the clouds invite me, like ghostly fingers, to come in now and take a load off.

Beyond the gate is a door, unlike any door I've ever seen. The door is not attached to anything. It's suspended in the air. No walls securing it. No frame

CHAPTER 2

holding it in place. It looks to be made of wood, but it's not like any wood I've ever seen. It's pale white with three equal sides. Each side is distinct but equal to the others. Three parts, yet one shape. In the center is a crystal knob.

I look back at the tree, then at the door, then back at the tree again, and I let go. I free my hands from the sting of the rope. For the first time in my life I feel free—free to make a choice—the rope or the door? I know what the tree has in store; a painful and humiliating death. The door, on the other hand, poses possibility.

What do I have to lose? What's behind door number one can't be any worse than what's behind the suicide tree over there, smiling, waiting for me. What waits for me on the other side of this door can't be any worse than what waits for me in hell.

Chapter 3

They that are in hell think there is no heaven.
—English proverb

I sit on a short gold bench along the wall at the end of a long hallway. The stark white walls meld into the stark white floors, and five more gold benches like the one I'm sitting on line the walls of the hallway. With the exception of a single doorway on the opposite wall at the other end of the hall, all the walls are bare. In the air, I detect the faint smell of incense.

I look around. Light is emanating from somewhere, but for the life of me I can't tell from where. The soft glow lighting the room looks like it may be coming from a skylight, but a quick glance at a white ceiling proves otherwise.

My eyes burn as they adjust to the glare. I'm filled with excitement, but I'm not sure why. I don't remember sitting down. The last thing I remember is walking through that gate and opening the door. I don't know how long I've been sitting, and I have no

CHAPTER 3

indication of how much longer I will sit. I'm just here.

The door at the end of the hall opens and closes quickly, but no one enters or exits. The only sound I hear is the man to my left tapping his foot. I look up at him, he looks down at me.

"Hello," I say as I extend my right hand.

"Cain," he replies with a good firm handshake. "Marked wanderer."

"Cain of Eden? The world's first birth? That Cain?"

Cain nodded, lowering his eyebrows. He smiled slightly. "That's me."

"My mother used to read to me every night from this big blue book of Bible stories. I loved those stories. I must have heard your story a hundred times. Noah and the ark, Moses and the Ten Commandments, Jonah and the whale." I smiled. "Man, it's an honor to meet you."

Cain nods humbly. "Thank you. I appreciate you not revisiting my shame."

I do have one question, though, if you don't mind me asking.

"What's that?"

"Why was your sacrifice not accepted by God?"

"It's complicated."

"I understand. Just let the past be the past. Brother, we all have something shameful in our past. I'm Judas."

Cain is calm when he answers. "I know who you are. We *all* know who you are."

I glance around the room. "Who is 'we'?"

Cain grins.

"And where are we?"

"Purgatory," a stunningly gorgeous woman down the hall answers from her bench without so much as looking up at me from filing her finger nails.

"Who's that?" I whisper to Cain.

"Queen Bathsheba."

"Uriah's wife?"

"David's *queen*," she responds quickly but without malice.

"My apologies, Queen," I offer. "Did she mean it when she said we're in purgatory?"

Cain nods.

I look around the room. "I imagined it would be more…colorful."

"It may have been. But you've already been purged. Now you're awaiting trial."

"Trial? You mean you've been waiting here for thousands of years to go to trial?"

"There are no years here—just the present. And I've been to trial several times; hung jury."

"Hung jury, huh? Doesn't it feel a little like you're still wandering?"

CHAPTER 3

"You have no idea."

"I'll have to get used to that no time thing," I say. "I hope you don't find this rude, but—"

Before I can even ask, Cain turns around to show me the back of his head where, from his ears back, his hair is blood red. "People always think it's going to be on my face. The mark covers my head."

"Hmm."

I retreat into my own thoughts. I suppose I'm grateful I don't remember the *purging* part of purgatory. Purging is only a good thing when expressed as a blues song or some other art form. I don't know how long I've been gone, but one thing I'm sure of: On earth below my death mattered to no one—and I mean no one! No one cried for me. No one came looking for me. After not seeing me around town for a few weeks no one even bothered to ask, "Has anyone seen Judas lately?" I suppose it makes sense. My existence was futile. My life wasn't like that of the apostle John or Paul. I didn't leave behind letters for future generations to *ooh* and *aww* over. The only thing my life produced was entire nations of people who hate me...and the loss of a man who was sent here to save those nations.

Come to think of it, after the gossip died down about what happened to Jesus in the garden, nobody really mentioned me again. When I *was* mentioned… well, you know the story. It's nothing to brag about.

These days, the only people who inquire about me are historians, theologians, and rebellious kids with black fingernails. They focus more on what I did than who I was, but at least I come to mind. The others—the good people of the world—aren't curious. They take the traditional stories at face value. Even if they do possess a little curiosity, they never admit to the fact that they have questions: Who was Judas, really? How did he live? Why did he do it? Did he go to heaven—or straight to hell?

It's that last one that's on my mind right now. What's going to happen at this so-called trial? Could I land in heaven? After all the pain and suffering I've caused, could I somehow end up in heaven? Geez louise! Who would drop the ball on that one? I mean, I'm Judas. No mother in her right mind has ever named her child after me. And who could blame her! To give a child my name, would, well, be sentencing that child to a life that was jinxed—forever!

I have stopped being a man and have become only a quality, a treacherous adjective. People label me as one of history's most despised villains, placing me in the same category as Hitler, Jesse James, and Lex Luthor.

CHAPTER 3

They forget I am a real person, that I have feelings, that I arrived on earth the same way the rest of us did—by way of a mother and a father.

I am one of the original twelve apostles for goodness' sake! Jesus chose me! Not the other way around. He said that I and the other eleven would sit on twelve thrones and judge the twelve tribes of Israel. When he sent us out to heal the sick and do miracles in his name, I was there with the rest of them. When the Lord kneeled to wash the disciples' feet, he washed my feet too! For all the talk, all the hatred, all the stories, people don't seem to understand me at all.

My name means *the praised one*, not the hated one—Google it.

I'm not a criminal.

I'm not a monster.

What I am is…misunderstood.

***

"Judas Iscariot," a woman's voice calls from inside the open door at the end of the hall.

I sigh and stand. "Cain, I have enjoyed our time together," I say as I pat the back of Adam and Eve's first-born son. I walk down the hall and pause in front of the queen.

"Godspeed, Judas Iscariot," she says.

Down the stark white hallway I walk as the thick gold-plated door slowly swings to a close behind me. I expect to enter a courtroom but have instead entered another room. One that is pitch-black. Like a cave dweller, I move about in this mansion with many rooms on all fours. I eventually find a door that is unlocked. I open it…and…applause erupts. What's going on? Fish-flying kites, saints skipping rope, children endlessly pouring sweets and chocolates down their mouths, it is the most wild and wondrous thing anyone could ever imagine.

Cherubs sing while flashing, dashing about. Kittens, rabbits, chipmunks—they all run out to look. Reared back on their hind legs they point at me and wave their paws. Handel's "Messiah" blasts in the background; skating fairies glide back and forth across the clouds; everything is electric—"Judas the Misunderstood has arrived," I overhear someone or something say.

I expected a courtroom of haters and instigators. Not this. This is too unbelievable. Mythological heroes competing against one another to win the grand prize—a chance to wash *my* feet? Young seraphim with eyes of diamond and six, gold-laced wings rush out to greet me. I will never forget the surreal sound of their

CHAPTER 3

wings and the sympathetic look in their eyes. A new chant thrives across the universe. A million voices fill the air and reach the throne of the Most High—God knows I'm here.

"Judas the Misunderstood, the Judge is ready for you," a voice calls. A hush falls over the crowd and I stand very still. Judge? As in my day of *judg*ment? Cain did say it would happen.

My old friend Matthew lays his hand on my shoulder. Our eyes meet and he nods once and winks. Granted, it's the nervous tic of a guy that spent his life collecting taxes for Caesar, but it's a wink nevertheless and I am encouraged. I move toward the double doors that lead to the courtroom. My newfound fan club follows behind in silence. I'm both comforted and racked with anxiety.

The first thing I see as I enter the courtroom is Father Abraham. He is both old and forever young. He is leaning against a boulder-sized pearl. Upon seeing me, he comes over and extends to me—Judas—the right hand of fellowship.

"Peace be with you," Abraham says and smiles. He squints when he smiles, but he cannot hide the wisdom of his time-worn face.

An angel guides me to my seat and my fan club fills

the row of seats directly behind me.

I sit in silence. Michael the Archangel kneels by my side. "The court has not pronounced judgment," he whispers into my ear. "Take heart. Do not be afraid. You've been accused, but there's not a lawyer anywhere, dead or alive, who will be able to make the charges stick."

My eyes enlarge with surprise. I feel foolish but grateful. Armed with a sword, Michael returns to the corner of the courtroom. Suddenly he lays down his sword and picks up a twelve-string guitar to pluck out a rendition of "Stairway to Heaven" that catches me totally off guard, and I start to hum along. Whatever this is—heaven, a dream—I like it.

Everyone stands and I turn in my seat to find out what the commotion is all about. Moses moves slowly into the courtroom. He smiles at me as he approaches, then grabs me in his arms and hangs on like he's catching up with an old war buddy for the first time. He then sits in the empty seat directly behind me.

Did Moses really just hug me? *The* Moses? The "Ten Commandments, thou shalt not kill" Moses? I wonder if he really has a stutter. Note to self: *If you survive whatever comes next, talk to Moses over dinner.* Also, don't forget to ask him how he squirmed out of being convicted for the Egyptian he killed. Any advice might be helpful.

I fix my mind on the case. I don't even know what the case is. I don't know whether I'll have to give an account. I don't know anything. And the fear I had been distracted from moments before returns with a vengeance. Fear is an old ally of mine. It protects my heart. Hold on to your fear and never let it go, my Sunday school teacher used to say, but she forgot to tell us that holding on to anything for too long is like holding your breath—you suffocate your essence.

I do wish I had understood Jesus better when we were back on earth. I guess I was too preoccupied with my own wants and needs. I probably would have made a good dictator, given half a chance…

I come out of my thoughts again just in time to notice a chubby-faced, cherry-cheeked angel staring at me. When I look at him, he flutters over to me and hovers so close, we're nose-to-nose for a few seconds. I'm not sure what the protocol is here. I don't have an arsenal of etiquette for dealing with angels. I turn the corners of my mouth up to feign a smile. He blushes and turns his face away from mine, but seconds later, I see out of my peripheral vision that he's looking at me, again. He's mesmerized, I think, by me, of all things.

Chapter 4

Wrong judgment is due to inadequate defense.
—Philippine proverb

I let my gaze dance around the room and take in as much as I can in just a few quick glimpses. The floors and walls of the courtroom are polished marble, inset with blue diamonds and rubies. The ceiling is solid gold. Floor-to-ceiling shelves are filled with books on every subject imaginable, from dinosaur anatomy to lost fairy tales to the history of planets. The room is beyond imagination, seeming more beautiful with each glance.

The piercing blare of horns sounds from the doors at the back of the courtroom and Michael stands.

"She is the one promised to succeed the Lord after his ascension. She was there in the beginning, hovering above the waters of the earth in the moments before time began. She manifested as wind in the upper room and gave the apostles the ability to speak in diverse tongues. You know her as the Advocate, the Spirit that

CHAPTER 4

intercedes on your behalf when you don't know what to pray for. Please welcome...the Holy Spirit."

Applause breaks out and I turn in my seat only slightly to catch a glimpse of her, but I don't see her. Suddenly, just before my eyes, a light zooms toward me from the courtroom doors, hovers, disappears then reappears even brighter than before. The twinkling zips past me, and a trail of wind opens up the path behind her, expanding to fill the courtroom.

"He was the Son of the Morning who led the rebellion in heaven and who took a third of the angels with him. He was beautiful. He was smart. His body was music. Now, he roams the earth seeking someone to devour. You know him as the Devil. He is the tempter, the accuser of the brethren. Make way for...Lucifer."

The doors fly open and two pools of a viscous black liquid spill into the courtroom. The smell of sulfur stings my nose and two beings that I can't quite identify form up from the liquid. They wear an armor of some kind, identifying them as soldiers, but they have tails, too many arms, and too many legs...

Then a thick black cloud whirls into the room and the low rumble of Lucifer's presence conjures up a sense of foreboding, doom, and gloom in my mind. A form stands in the cloud as the fog funnels around him. The echo of the rattling made by the whirlwind takes my breath for a moment. "I th-th-think I am going to fa-fa-faint."

I turn my face away from him just as he turns to look at me, and I focus my attention on the Holy Spirit.

I'm so shaken I do not hear the bailiff summon me to the witness stand. An angel lifts me out of my seat and flies me, unaware, across the room, placing me in a huge mahogany chair in the courtroom's center. All eyes are on me.

Michael speaks again. "All rise."

And we do.

The archangel continues, "The Alpha and the Omega. The Righteous Judge. The Holy One. Giver of immortal gladness. Come, bow down and worship the Lord, our Maker—the Honorable I AM that I AM."

I can't look, not directly anyway. God's presence is so immense and intoxicating that my attempts to worship are hindered by my inability to stand or think. He's just…awesome. I eventually join in with the angels and my newfound fan club in the singing of the hymn, "Holy! Holy! Holy!" I like the song, but how long we sing it for—singing it over and over again—is anyone's guess.

CHAPTER 4

Finally, our worship ends, and I feel a soft, breezy, whimsical movement making its way through the courtroom with a fragrance so charming and pure, even the accusing faces of the prosecuting team brighten. The Holy Spirit, my Advocate, begins to speak with a voice as sweet as honey:

"His name," my Advocate begins, "displaces him just as a factory worker is displaced by cutbacks in a big corporation."

I wonder what in the world she is talking about.

"Never," continues the Advocate, "has he cursed God. Never has he intentionally stirred the pot. Never has he held his head high in pride. Like Job, he persevered in faith in the face of unfathomable challenges."

The Judge interrupts the Advocate. "No excessive speech-making please; just the facts."

"He was circumcised on the eighth day," the Advocate says. "The clumsy, one-handed doctor his mother hired to circumcise him couldn't stop the bleeding. Let me rephrase that. He wasn't a doctor, he was a butcher! I have the proof."

"Objection," the Accuser hisses. "This has nothing to do with the case at hand."

"On the contrary, it shows a man who has been bogged down by an uphill battle since the day he was born," says the Advocate.

"Allowed," the Judge says. "Go on."

"Here is a soul misunderstood. His father died when he was just entering adulthood. His stepfather abused him physically and emotionally. When Jesus found him, he was a broken young man, angry, hurting, and unable to trust anyone."

"Nice. Playing the blame game, huh? 'My grandma spanked me.' 'Daddy didn't tuck me in at night.' 'Mommy never gave me Band-Aids for my boo-boos.' Come on, now. This is beneath even Judas," the Accuser calls out.

"Counsel," the Judge warns, "get to your point."

"The point is he did his best. This man was ignored for most of his life. The only friendships he ever formed were with Jesus and the other apostles. Yet we expect him to come into an intimate situation like that and immediately know how to love. It just doesn't work that way."

"The way in which he matured doesn't excuse the betrayal," says the Accuser.

Betrayal. I have come to loathe that word…

The Accuser continues, "Do you now deny he had the Son of Man murdered?"

"Original sin put him on the cross—not Judas," the

CHAPTER 4

Advocate replies. You know like I do the Son had to lay his life down. At no point did Judas ever have the authority to take life. Judas wasn't being malicious. In fact, he didn't even realize he was going to play such an important part in the salvation of the world. He was just a man doing what he thought was right."

The Accuser smiles. "You know what they say: The road to hell is paved with good intentions."

The Judge chimes in. "You will refrain from commentary, Lucifer."

"This is a man who spent his childhood working without complaint. This is a man who found his strength and his voice—a passion he was born with. Zealous pride and loyalist behavior were in his DNA. This is a man who would have died in Christ's place for the good of the cause, given half a chance. He is not a villain."

Tears well in my eyes and roll down my cheeks. *I'm not a villain. I'm not.*

"Judge, you know like I do who is responsible for the actions that led to the crucifixion. The Son's death wasn't a surprise. It wasn't some unexpected misfortune which befell him. It was your perfect, eternal will, and he knew it would come to that. He had to die in order for the scriptures to be fulfilled."

The Judge responds. "The fact that certain scriptures have been fulfilled doesn't exonerate him of guilt, Counsel."

"No, it doesn't, sir. But you made him to be entrepreneurial, a risk taker. You intended for him to be the voice of a generation. The mistreated, the outcast, the uneducated boy who grew up as his stepfather's punching bag is one of the twelve chosen to rule and to reign with the Son of Man. He should be a judge, not a defendant."

I don't believe what I'm hearing.

"Isn't this the one who has been damned for all time?" the serpent asks.

"This is eternity, Counsel," the Judge reminds. "Not time."

The Accuser leaps from his seat. "Your Honor—Judas stole from the purse. He kept secrets. He made a deal with the enemies and he took the pay-off. Not to mention his final act of cowardice, which he would have surely carried out if you hadn't graciously offered him another option, that damn door."

"Watch your mouth, Lucifer. I will have none of that up here," the Judge scolds.

"But he didn't commit suicide," the Advocate said quickly.

CHAPTER 4

I swallow hard at the idea that the Judge and everyone else listening may think of me as a coward, and before I can stop the words, I hear myself whisper, "I'm not a coward."

The Accuser looks over at me then at the Judge.

"Judas Iscariot," the Judge begins, "do you have something to say?"

"I'm not a coward," I say a little louder.

"If you believe that, I've got a bridge to sell you," the Accuser says.

I retreat into myself again. This experience reminds me of the last time I saw my family. My stepfather had been drinking and my mother was getting the worst of his self-hate that night. I got tired of hearing her screams. Tired of the thumps. I rose up with a sharpened stake to defend her honor. Only she didn't think she had any honor worth defending. I stood up to him. "No more hitting," I said while wedging myself between them, shielding my mother behind me. "He won't hurt you anymore, Mom," I said. But my words fell to the ground then, and they seem to be meeting the same fate now in this courtroom. Instead of hiding behind me as I fought him off, my mother turned on me. My stepfather got a few forceful jabs in before he dragged me out of the house, locking the door behind me.

In the month it took me to find a job after my stepfather kicked me out of the house, I was homeless. People never seem to understand that homeless is not the same as useless. I begged for food and twice reached the point of starvation. I didn't want to steal. Before my father died, he taught me that stealing was wrong, that the Lord would have no part in helping a thief. But it was steal or it was starve. So I stole.

My attention shifts back to the Advocate's voice.

"He never understood why his journey never got any easier as time went on. Why he could never maintain a smile for more than a day. Why he could never become carefree and full of happiness like the people he watched through the coffee shop window. Why he could never stop worrying about what struggle would come at him next.

"Judge, think of all the times he worked for pay but then wasn't paid fairly. Think of all the times he went to the deli and never came home with what he ordered. Think of all the times he went to the barber shop and left with his hair uneven. Think of all the times he reached out to the people around him for support and understanding only to be shunned and rejected.

"Judge, you know how bad it was. He had no family support, had rocks thrown at him by children, was even spat upon by strangers. Bathed in a cold sweat, crushed under the weight he was carrying, you know all the times he stood at the edge of that bridge, bawling his eyes out, ready to jump, ready to give in and give up."

"Thank you for the stroll down memory lane," the Judge interjects, "but I know his steps and what he went through. Let me remind you that we're not here to rehash the life and times of Judas Iscariot. His road has been no different from any other man's road. As the good book says, he was given nothing more than what he could handle."

"But, Judge, even when he did play along with the team of twelve and do what was expected of him, he was still misunderstood and mistreated. Sure, they went along with him, but they talked about him behind his back. Perhaps it had something to do with him being the only one in the group not from Galilee, but from Judah. Perhaps it had something to do with him being appointed treasurer, the most trusted position in the group. Perhaps it had something to do with him sitting next to the host, in the spot of the most honored guest at the Last Supper."

"So?" the Accuser interrupts.

"So Jesus could have easily stopped him," my Advocate continues. "All he had to do was tell the others what Judas was planning, that he was going to hand him over to the Romans, and he would have never left the room alive. But he didn't. Judas got to have one last meal with his best friend and trusted teacher. People don't understand that what he wanted wasn't 30 pieces of silver. He wanted his friend to lead a revolution. He wanted more fellowship, more time with Jesus to develop strategies together and fight the good fight. That's what he wanted.

"The cross Judas had to bear was too much for one man to handle. But he did what the world needed him to do. The life he lived was plain. The words he lived by were simple: *Forgive them, Lord, for they do not know what they are doing*.

"Judas did what was required. He wanted someone to love him, not hate him. He wanted to be trusted, not doubted. Judas would have done anything for Jesus. Even turn him over to the authorities. He was the only one of the twelve with strength enough to do what Jesus needed him to do. He's not a devil. He's a hero."

Chapter 5

God does not pay weekly, but pays at the end.
—Dutch proverb

After the Advocate's eloquent final plea, the word "hero" still echoes in my mind. Silence fills the courtroom and we all wait for the Judge's decision. A few tense moments pass as a stern, powerful voice breaks through the silence following the Advocate's final words.

"Ladies and gentlemen of the jury," the Judge begins. "I have the verdict"—but stops short…

"Ladies and gentlemen," the Judge begins again, this time softer, but once more he interrupts himself.

And at last, an even more subdued voice emerged as the Judge, Lord God Almighty, continues with his decision. "Judas," he says, "You did not betray Jesus but did what he needed you to do. You were the first star, the one who cracked open the door to life more abundant. You're the only one my son trusted. It was your shadow that brightened the dawn. It was your commitment that made way for Jesus' Cross and Crown. Fret not that you are misunderstood—you will always be misunderstood—and so will I."

Profound silence engulfs the courtroom.

Then, from out of nowhere, a new voice. One that is different, but oddly familiar. I don't immediately recognize who's speaking. "Judas," it says as it hangs in the air and wafts in the stillness in a way that brings me a measure of peace. The same kind of calm I used to feel back on earth whenever Jesus would speak to me. The voice continues, "Judas, my child, you are my miracle."

It *is* Jesus. And my heart begins to weep. I want to raise my eyes but they are full of tears. By now he's only a few inches in front of me. I want to look at him but I can't stop myself from sobbing. Never has any man felt such joy in weeping. For the first time I feel like someone truly understands me. I searched my whole life for love, and it turns out I had it all along—with Jesus—I am accepted—flaws and all.

"Judas," Jesus says, "I saw your suffering. I heard your pleas for the suffering to end. But you had to say yes to suffering before you could transcend it. There is not a limb in your body that is whole, not a corner of your heart that has not hardened, not an inch of your soul that is not bleeding—and you have never been understood. On earth below, guilt is your idol. There was a thief inside you. On earth below, people believe that *the fall* of man means you must always look down when in reality it is a story of awakening, and thus the beginning of *looking up*. Up here is the real world. Up here you will see things differently. Up here you will eat the bread and drink from the cup. Up here you will feast on a banquet of unconditional love. The court has no cause to pass sentence against you.

"All the praise you now hear is only the reverse echo of your own misunderstood life. I withheld extravagance from you on earth below, but now it is yours to enjoy. All the comfort you now receive is only the embrace of your own misunderstood kiss. All the camaraderie you now have is only the reflection of your own misunderstood coin-tossing change of heart. All the love you now feel is only the prison of your own earthly body setting you free. Of all the words you now hear, *impossible*, now do you see, is but another word for *grace*."

Jesus extends the right hand of fellowship and smiles that same quirky smile he would smile when he thought of something clever to say back on earth.

Without warning, he kisses me!

Warm light instantly streams in from every corner of the room. Six points of light shine on me and I am filled with peace and love. All fear is gone. In every place where I had pain on earth, there is now happiness. In every place where I hid uncertainty, there is now assurance.

"Jesus, are you welcoming *me* with a kiss?" I ask.

Jesus grins. "Welcome home, friend. I imagine our magnum opus is, and will always be, one and the same—misunderstood."

Closing Letter from the Author

Friend,

Thank you for pushing through to the end. I do hope you found this story entertaining. Most of all, I pray that it prodded you to think outside the box (even if it was just for a moment).

Whether you read to the end simply to get your money's worth, or read each line hoping to find the presence of a clearly defined deceptive undercurrent, whether you took notes or turned away in disgust vowing to never read this again, know that I applaud you reading on nonetheless.

If you happen to have enjoyed this fiction-filled tall tale, I invite you to read on just a bit further. You might just find what you're searching for. Maybe even discover a few things you didn't know you were searching for.

With a forgiving heart,
Jason E. Royle

It Is Written

Everything must be fulfilled that is written about me in the Law of Moses, the Prophets and the Psalms.
—Luke 24:44

Whether the betrayal came by the hands of Judas or by someone else, it most certainly would come. In order for Old Testament prophecies to be true, the things that happened to Jesus had to happen or they wouldn't be considered *a fulfillment* of prophecy—"the Scriptures must be fulfilled," Jesus said.

Jesus had to be betrayed and handed over—it is written:

<u>As Jesus said</u>:

> *"The Son of Man will go just as it is written about him."* (Matthew 26:24a)

> *"This has all taken place so that the writings of the prophets might be fulfilled."* (Matthew 26:56)

"The Son of Man must be delivered into the hands of sinful men, be crucified and on the third day be raised again." (Luke 24:7)

"I have not lost one of those you gave me." (John 18:9b)

"This is to fulfill the scripture: 'He who shares my bread has lifted up his heel against me.'" (John 13:18–19; the prophecy Jesus refers to is Psalm 41:9.)

As Peter said:

"Friends, the Scripture had to be fulfilled which the Holy Spirit spoke long ago through the mouth of David concerning Judas, who served as guide for those who arrested Jesus—he was one of our number and shared in this ministry." (Acts 1:15-17)

As Paul said:

King Agrippa, "I am saying nothing beyond what the prophets and Moses said would happen—that the Christ would suffer and, as the first to rise from the dead, would proclaim light to his own people and to the Gentiles." (Acts 26:22b-23)

<u>As Zechariah said</u>:

> *"I told them, 'If you think it best, give me my pay; but if not, keep it.' So they paid me thirty pieces of silver. And the Lord said to me, 'Throw it into the potter'—the handsome price at which they priced me! So I took the thirty pieces of silver and threw them into the house of the Lord to the potter."* (Zechariah 11:12-13; the fulfillment of this prophecy is documented in Matthew 27:9 as a combination of references to the prophets Zechariah and Jeremiah.)

***

There should be no lingering doubt about whether Jesus was "delivered into the hands of sinful men." By way of Judas or by someone else, it was going to happen—if not—*"how, then, would the Scriptures be fulfilled that say it must happen in this way?"* (Matthew 26:54).

The Devil Made Me Do It

"The devil-made-me do it."

Comedian Flip Wilson may have breathed new life into that popular phrase with his hilarious character, Geraldine Jones, but I honestly think the circumstances surrounding Judas gave birth to that phrase. The Gospels of Luke and John specifically point to the fact that Judas was under the direction of Satan when he handed Jesus over (Luke 22:3 and John 13:2, 27).

John's Gospel reads: *"As soon as Judas took the bread, Satan entered into him."*

Satan entered into him. Now that doesn't seem very fair. Poor Judas didn't stand a chance. I guess the Devil really did have a role to play in the events that led to Jesus' death on a cross. If you want someone to blame, blame him—the Devil—not Judas. He's the one who did it.

No matter how credentialed or uncredentialed you may be, you would be hard pressed not to agree with one plain, simple fact—the Devil had a hand in what Judas did.

Of further interest is the fact that the Greek translation of John 13:27 has two basic forms of scholarly interpretation:

(1) The Devil put it into Judas' heart to betray Jesus, or

(2) The Devil resolved in his own heart that Judas should do it.

Either way you look at it, Judas was a tool (or a victim, depending on your perspective) used by Satan to bring about what he no doubt thought was the destruction of Jesus.

Some will argue that Jesus was protecting the apostles from Satan, and once Jesus stopped protecting Judas, Satan entered into him, and that Judas had a choice and that he chose betrayal over friendship with God.

Here, again, no matter how you look at it, Jesus *allowed* Judas to be tempted by withdrawing his protection from him so that Satan could enter into him. Jesus had a mission to fulfill, and if that meant one of his disciples would have to betray him to set the wheels of world reconciliation into motion, then so be it.

The real question we should be asking ourselves is not, "Why did Judas do it?" but rather, "Why did God allow Satan to do what he did?"

The Betrayer(s)

During the Last Supper, Jesus declared that one of the twelve would betray him. There was great confusion at this. The disciples were puzzled. Clearly no one other than Jesus knew it would be Judas (Matthew 26:22; Mark 14:19; Luke 22:23; John 13:22).

In Mark's account (Mark 14:19), for example, one after another all the disciples ask, "I'm not the one, am I?" They could not picture themselves as sheep who would desert their shepherd, but later that same night Jesus warns all of them (Mark 14:27):

- "You will all lose faith" (REB)
- "Become deserters" (NRSV)
- "Fall away" (NIV)

But each one fiercely pledges his allegiance to Jesus, even in the face of death (Mark 14:31b). But before the night is over, as predicted, *all* of them turn their backs on Jesus (Mark 14:50), not just Judas, but every last one of them.

What Mark's Gospel has done in this brief but eye-opening nugget of information is pushed all of us to carefully consider one very important, very personal question:

Who, then, is not a betrayer?

The Way of Judas

The path laid out for Jesus and the path laid out for Judas are as different as night and day. And yet, in the end, they merge to bring about the same result—Jesus' death, burial, and resurrection.

"The way" of the Cross is a celebrated symbol that leads us by sparks of light into the vast tomorrow. If today you're not okay, set your sights on what God may do for you—tomorrow.

"The way" of Judas, on the other hand, pushes us to confront any and every morsel of darkness found within—today. Tomorrow may be too late, so you better make it right with God today.

Doesn't it make you wonder? Could it be that we don't really hate Judas as much as we fear "the way" of Judas? We don't like dealing with the darkness within, not today anyway. We would rather ignore it, take care of it later, maybe tomorrow.

So there you have it. We fear the way of Judas more than we fear the way of the Cross. Why? Well, because, in the end, the way of the Cross is a battle that has already been won. What we fear most is the day-to-day struggle with who we really are.

WE are Judas.

***

"Let he who is without sin cast the first stone," Jesus said to them. At this, those who heard began to go away one at a time, until only Jesus was left with the woman still standing there. "Where are they?" Jesus said to her. "Has no one condemned you?" "No one, sir," she said. "Then neither do I condemn you," Jesus declared. (John 8:7-11)

Suicide in the Bible

The attitude toward suicide in the bible ranges from vagueness to nobility. Surprisingly, none of the examples of suicide found in the bible make any specific, unfavorable comments about the *ethics* of suicide. This does not mean the bible endorses suicide. It just means that this is an interesting, lesser known fact.

There are seven examples of suicide found in the bible:

Samson – Braced between two pillars, he used his final strength to push them down, and take his own life along with his enemies. (Judges 16:25-30)

Abimelech – After a certain woman dropped a millstone on his head, Abimelech ordered his armor-bearer to draw his sword and kill him so that no one could say "a woman killed him." (Judges 9:50-55)

King Saul – Because of defeat by the enemy and great fear after being wounded, Saul chose to end his life rather than face his captors. (1 Sam. 31:3-5)

Saul's Armor-Bearer – Out of hopelessness and terror after seeing that Saul was dead, this assistant to the king impulsively took his life as well. (1 Sam. 31:5)

Ahithophel – As a one-time close companion of David, and grandfather of Bathsheba, Ahithophel eventually took up the cause of Absalom's rise against him. But when he noticed that his advice had not been taken to lead to final defeat over David's army, out of possible fear, rejection, or complete hopelessness, he chose to go home, "put his house in order, and then hanged himself." (2 Sam. 17:23)

Zimri – As an evil king of Israel and facing utter defeat, Zimri saw no way out, except to take his own life. He set the palace on fire and died in it, rather than face his enemy. (1 Kings 16:15-20)

Judas – "When Judas saw that Jesus was condemned, he repented and brought back the thirty pieces of silver…and he went and hanged himself." (Mt. 27:3-5)

SUICIDE IN THE BIBLE

***

It is the belief of some Christians that because a person cannot ask for forgiveness after suicide that it will forever separate them from God's love. But there are *many* sins which may never be confessed before one's death.

The bible reminds us that when we are in Christ nothing will separate us from God, not even death. "For I am convinced that neither death, nor life, nor angels, nor principalities, nor things present, nor things to come, nor powers, nor height, nor depth, nor any other created thing, will be able to separate us from the love of God, which is in Christ Jesus our Lord" (Rom. 8:38-39).

Suicide is a sin. There is no doubt about that. It is self-murder. But is it worse than all the other evils? Is it unpardonable? Are you still saved? Does it determine a person's eternal destiny?

> Nowhere in the bible does it say
> the act of suicide is an unforgivable sin.

The bible tells us the only sin which cannot be forgiven is blasphemy against the Holy Spirit. "And so I tell you, <u>every kind of sin</u> and slander <u>can be forgiven</u>, but blasphemy against the Spirit will not be forgiven" (Mt. 12:31).

Since the bible does not speak about the eternal consequences of suicide, why should we presume to understand what happens to people after death by their own hand? In reality, only God knows the fate of each soul who comes before the judgment seat.

***

Let's take a closer look at Judas' suicide for a moment. Arguably, the author of the Gospel of Matthew intends for the reader to interpret Judas' hanging as an act of remorse. Judas repents (*metamelētheis*), returns the money he received for turning Jesus over to the authorities, and acknowledges that he has "sinned in betraying innocent blood" (Mt. 27:3-4).

If Judas knew that he had sinned in betraying innocent blood, that is to his credit. He did not hide his sin. He is nobler in his death than Caiaphas and Pilate in their arrogant loftiness. With Matthew we see that scripture is fulfilled even while those fulfilling it are driven by guilt and shame to their own self-destruction.

As noted by some scholars, Judas' suicide may be interpreted as an *act of atonement* because he himself carries out the penalty laid down in the Hebrew Bible for taking a life: "atonement cannot be made for the land on which blood has been shed, except by the blood of the one who shed it" (Num 35:33; see also Lev 24:17).

There is no hint of eternal damnation or condemnation of Judas' self-killing in Matthew. If anything, it is a solution to his guilt rather than something that adds to it.

The Last Supper Betrayal: What Really Happened?

It is remarkable that Judas Iscariot is not mentioned by name in Mark and Luke's account of the Last Supper. And there is no reference in the *synoptic* gospels to the fact that Judas left the room before the interpretation of the significance of the meal, nor is he identified in Mark and Luke as the betrayer by Jesus. Matthew identifies the betrayer as merely "Judas" (no Iscariot; Mt. 26:25-27).

Only **JOHN** identifies him as *"Judas Iscariot, son of Simon,"* and only John indicates, *"as soon as Judas had taken the bread, he went out"* (Jn. 13:26, 30).

MARK described Jesus' betrayer as, *"the one dipping (bread?) into the bowl with me."* Which probably indicates that Judas stretched forth his hand at the same moment as Jesus in a gesture declaring that he rejected Jesus' leadership (Mk. 14:20). The Greek lacks the word "bread."

MATTHEW wrote, *"the one who has dipped his hand into the bowl with me"* (Mt. 26:21-23). According to S.T. Lach's "Rabbinic Commentary on the NT," all the men will dip their bread into the sauce bowl at one time or another during the meal. For Matthew, the announcement serves primarily as a Christological function for the reader: Jesus knows his fate in advance—be delivered up to God, by means of Judas.

LUKE said, *"the hand of the one betraying me is with mine on the table"* (Lk. 22:21). Luke refers to Judas' betrayal <u>after</u> the Lord's Supper rather than before, why? Maybe Luke was seeking to teach his readers that mere participation in the Lord's Supper does not 'guarantee' membership in God's kingdom (Luke presented similar teachings elsewhere 8:4-15; 13:22-30; 14:16-24). More certain, however, is that he wanted his readers to ask themselves whether—as they share the Lord's Table—are they faithful disciples?

JOHN noted, *"the one whom I will give this piece of bread when I have dipped it in the dish."* In normal circumstances, the giving of the morsel (13:26) was a mark of favor; eating bread together was a sign of close friendship. Moreover, it would appear that Judas was seated in the place of honor since Jesus was able to hand him the piece of bread. We should take this portrayal of Jesus' action, then, as a sign of his friendship with Judas despite his knowledge of Judas' intentions. The remarkable thing John indicates is that still no one at the table fully realized what was happening. Judas' departure could have been for any reason, and there was no particular reason for the other disciples to connect it with the betrayal. Some thought that Jesus had sent him to buy food for the feast (which lasted for seven days), others that he had gone to carry out the customary practice of giving money to the poor (Jn. 13:29).

Works Consulted

Beasley-Murray, George R. *John: Word Biblical Commentary, Vol. 36, Second Edition*. Nashville, TN: Thomas Nelson, 1999.

Klassen, William. *Judas: Betrayer or Friend of Jesus?* Minneapolis, MN: Fortress Press, 1996.

Lachs, Samuel T. *A Rabbinic Commentary on the New Testament: The Gospels of Matthew, Mark and Luke*. Hoboken, NJ: KTAV Publishing House, 1987.

Marshall, Alfred. *The Interlinear NRSV-NIV Parallel New Testament in Greek and English*. Grand Rapids, MI: Zondervan, 1993.

Robbins, Vernon. "Last Meal: Preparation, Betrayal, and Absence." *The Passion in Mark*, ed. Werner H. Kelber. Philadelphia, PA: Fortress Press, 1976.

Thank you for reading *Judas: Hero Misunderstood.*

Gaining exposure as an author relies heavily on word of mouth. Please consider leaving a short review wherever you can. It would be greatly appreciated.

—Jason E. Royle

Made in the USA
Middletown, DE
18 February 2020